Snapshots in American Black History

The Untold Stories of Courageous Americans in the Face of Unimaginable Obstacles

Jon Saboe

Outskirts Press, Inc.
Denver, Colorado

Snapshots in American Black History
The Untold Stories of Courageous Americans in the Face of Unimaginable Obstacles
All Rights Reserved
Copyright © 2007 Jon R. Saboe
v2.0

Outskirts Press
http://www.outskirtspress.com

ISBN-10: 1-4327-0627-6
ISBN-13: 978-1-4327-0627-2

Outskirts Press and the "OP" logo are trademarks belonging to Outskirts Press, Inc.

Printed in the United States of America

To a great Black-American, Daniel Edward Moore. An entrepreneur, restaurateur, Korean war veteran, husband, parent, business partner, and the greatest father-in-law in the world!

Content:

Introduction:

The purpose of these snapshots is to show the superiority of individual Black-Americans in morality, courage, and creativity when confronted by overwhelming odds. Much of these anecdotes deal with Civil War era politics, and a brief commentary is needed to demonstrate the high passions that ran on both sides of the slavery issue.

At the crux of the issue was the question of whether or not slavery was even wrong. On the one side were the Republicans who believed that slavery was immoral before God, and should be eliminated at any cost. They were regarded as religious extremists, imposing moralists, and "damned abolitionists". Violent activists were involved in armed raids of trains, boats, and courthouses to free slaves. (The "Operation Rescue" of the mid-1800s).

On the other side were Democrats who believed that slavery was completely justified. They cited world history as their example, and declared their right to privacy, property rights, and "State's Rights" as their defense. They claimed that the Constitution forbade the Federal Government from interfering with state laws concerning slavery; but this meant that blacks had to be re-categorized as non-viable or sub-human so that the Constitutional mandates against depriving a man of "life, liberty or property without due process" would not apply to the slave. As a result, much effort was made to convince the public that the slave was simply cattle and protected private property.

In the middle of the road was a party made up of statesmen who had left the Republican Party, and formed the Whig party. Their platform proclaimed the belief that slavery was wrong, but they also abhorred the imposition of that moral belief on others. They warned Republicans that slavery was an ugly fact of human existence and any attempt to thwart this natural order of things would lead to the demise of the Republican Party.

President Abraham Lincoln addressed this philosophy in the following speech, given in Connecticut in 1860.

"Let us apply a few tests. You say that you think slavery is wrong, but you denounce all attempts to restrain it. Is there anything else that you think wrong, that you are not willing to deal with as a wrong? Why are you so careful, so tender of this one wrong and no other? You will not let us do a single thing as if it were wrong; there is no place where you will allow it to be even wrong; there is no place where you will allow it even to be called wrong! We must not call it wrong in politics because that is bringing religion into politics; we must not call it wrong in the pulpit because that is bringing politics into religion...and there is no single place, according to you, where this wrong thing can be properly called wrong!"

In modern America, we replace the word 'slavery' with abortion.

Jon Saboe
1999

Chapter 1
The Real McCoy

Elijah McCoy was born in 1841 to parents who were runaway slaves from Kentucky. They escaped into Canada, but after the Civil War, they relocated to Michigan.

Elijah grew up watching and loving trains, and eventually went to Scotland to get a degree in Mechanical Engineering. When he returned to the States, however, he could not get a job doing anything pertaining to his degree, so he was eventually hired as an oilman for a train line.

Trains at that time had to stop every 100 miles and get "re-oiled". Elijah's job was to get out and oil every moving part of the train so it could move another 100 miles. He thought, "There must be a way to oil the train while it is moving," and he eventually designed a lubrication device that oiled the wheels and mechanical components without having to stop the train. He patented his invention, and soon made millions as train companies could now move products much faster and perishables could be shipped without spoiling.

Soon, competitors began to design their own lubricators, but the entire shipping industry soon dismissed anything that wasn't the "Real McCoy", because Elijah's design was so superior.

The next time you hear the phrase "The Real McCoy", remember where it came from.

Chapter 2
"The pursuit of the difficult makes men strong."

Edward Brooke was born in Washington DC in 1919, and was named after his father who was a V.A. Lawyer. He received an undergraduate from Howard University, but was undecided about whether to pursue Law or Medicine.

He was drafted into World War II as a Second Lieutenant because of his education. His duties were supposed to be confined to legal representation for enlisted men, but his regiment, (the 366th Combat Infantry Regiment) was shipped overseas and was eventually involved in the Italy invasion. Because he spoke fluent Italian, he infiltrated behind enemy lines in preparation for the invasion, masquerading as a Mussolini sympathizer from Africa. He received a Bronze Star for heroism.

After the invasion, he vacationed in Italy, and eventually married an Italian lady by the name of Remigia

Ferrari Scacco. They returned to the United States, and Brooke finished his Law Degree from Boston University in 1948—but wartime friends convinced Brooke to run for public office in Massachusetts; a state with a 5% black electorate.

In 1950 he lost his bid for state legislature.

In 1952 he lost his bid for general court judge.

In 1960 he lost his bid for Secretary of State, but he had been elected the chairman of the Boston Finance Commission and had become famous as a crusader against corruption.

In 1962 he barely won the State Attorney General office.

He then became a statewide symbol of honesty because of his assault on corruption, and was nominated by the Republican Party for the U.S. Senate in 1966. He won the election by a landslide, and became the first Black-American US Senator in the 20th century. (There had been several in the 1800's)

He was among the first Republican Senators to call for President Nixon's resignation.

"Those of us who serve in Congress...must do more than mirror the present fears and antagonisms of the electorate. We must do what we believe to be legally and morally right." Edward W. Brooke

Chapter 3
"Deeds of Valor"

A majority of the people coming to this country before the Revolutionary war came as indentured servants. Coming from England, Europe, and Africa, they formed an interracial sub-culture which had come to America in exchange for seven years of work. The armies of the Revolutionary War were comprised of these new Americans.

Early one spring day in 1782, a young black lady named Deborah Gannett disguised herself as a man and, under the pseudonym 'Robert Shurtliff', she registered with the Massachusetts Militia. Under this pretense she served with the Revolutionary Armies for more than eighteen months without detection, until receiving her (his) honorable discharge.

After the war, however, her deceit led to difficulties receiving her pay, until a resolution was passed and presented to the Massachusetts courts on her behalf for

"Deeds of Valor". It read:

On of the petition of Deborah Gannett, praying for compensation for services in the Continental Army, January 20, 1792. Whereas, it appears to this Court that the said Deborah Gannett enlisted, under the name of Robert Shurtliff, in Capt. Webb's company in the 4th Massachusetts Regiment, on May 20th 1782, and did actually perform the duty of a soldier, in the late army of the United States to the 23rd day of October, 1783 for which she received no compensation; and, whereas, it further appears that the said Deborah exhibited an extraordinary instance of female heroism, by discharging the duties of a faithful, gallant soldier, and at the same time preserving the virtue and chastity of her sex, unsuspected and unblemished, and was discharged from the service with fair and honorable character.

Once this evidence was presented to the courts, another resolution was written to assure Gannett's compensatory pay. The treasurer of the Commonwealth was directed to issue a *"note to the said Deborah for the sum of thirty-four pounds bearing interest from October 23, 1773"*.

Chapter 4
Benjamin Banneker

Benjamin Banneker was born in 1731, the son of Robert and Mary Bannaky. He grew up on the family farm, purchased by his grandmother after her seven years of indentured servitude expired. Around town it was known as "Bannaky Springs" due to the fresh water springs on the land. Benjamin used ditches and little dams to control the water from the springs for irrigation. His work was so reliable that the Bannaky's crops flourished even in dry spells. The family of free blacks raised good tobacco crops all the time.

Molly, Benjamin's grandmother, taught him and his brothers to read, using her Bible as a lesson book. There was no school in the valley for the boys to attend. Then one summer, a Quaker schoolteacher came to live in the valley. He set up a school for boys which Benjamin attended. The schoolmaster changed the spelling of his name to Banneker. At school he learned to write and do simple arithmetic.

When Banneker was twenty-one, a remarkable thing happened: he saw a patent watch. The watch belonged to a man named Josef Levi. Banneker was absolutely fascinated with the watch—he had never seen anything like it. Levi gave his watch to Banneker which was to change his life. Banneker took the watch apart to see how it worked. He carved similar watch pieces out of wood and made a large clock of his own; the first striking clock to be made completely in America. Banneker's clock was so precise it struck every hour, on the hour, for over forty years. His work on the clock led him to repair watches, clocks and sundials. Banneker even helped Joseph Ellicott to build a complex clock. Banneker became close friends with the Ellicott brothers. They lent him books on astronomy and mathematics as well as instruments for observing the stars. Banneker taught himself astronomy and advanced mathematics.

Banneker's parents died, leaving him the farm since his two sisters had married and moved away. Banneker built a "work cabin" with a skylight to study the stars and make calculations. Working largely alone, with few visitors, he compiled results which he published in his Almanac.

In 1792, President George Washington, on the recommendation of Secretary of State Thomas Jefferson, appointed Banneker to a six-member team to survey the "Federal Territory". Banneker and Ellicott worked closely with Pierre L'Enfant who was the architect in charge of planning Washington D.C.

L'Enfant was suddenly dismissed from the project due to his temper. When he left, he took the plans with him. Banneker recreated the plans from memory, saving the U.S. government the effort and expense of having someone else design the capital.

Although Banneker studied and recorded his results until he died, he stopped publishing his Almanac due to poor sales. His contributions to astronomy and mathematics caused President Thomas Jefferson to correspond with him regularly, and he always signed his letters, "your faithful servant and brother, Thos. Jefferson". Banneker died on Sunday, October 26, 1806. His gravestone marker can be found at Westchester Grade School, Oella Road and Westchester Ave., Oella, MD.

Chapter 5
Isn't he lovely?

On May 13, 1950, a premature black baby was placed in an incubator in Saginaw, Michigan. This baby was given too much oxygen, and although the baby lived, he was to suffer permanent blindness.

When he first started school, he was the only blind child in the classroom, and although very bright, he was shy to the point of autism, according to his first teacher.

One day a mouse began running around the classroom, disturbing class. Although this was not uncommon, the teacher and class could not locate the mouse to catch it or chase it out. The teacher finally asked the class to be completely quiet, and then told her sightless pupil that the other children's hearing wasn't as good as his. Could he please listen carefully and track the mouse so they could catch it? The little boy got down on all fours, and immediately located the mouse, chasing it outdoors.

He became an instant hero at school and all shyness and

autism vanished. He began to take great pride in his hearing and immediately picked up piano; followed by drums and harmonica, singing in the church choir, and listening to the music of Ray Charles and Sam Cooke.

Eventually, little Steveland Morris acquired the stage name Stevie Wonder, and the rest is history.

Chapter 6
Tireless Zeal

Blanche Kelso Bruce was born a slave on the Farmville Plantation, Virginia in 1841. He secretly received an education from his master's son's tutor. In 1861 he escaped to the free state of Kansas, and started an elementary school for blacks. After the Civil war, he studied at Oberlin College, until finances forced him to take a porter job on a riverboat.

In 1869 he traveled to Mississippi with 75 cents in his pocket. His hard work and winning personality led him to success as a tax assessor, sheriff, school superintendent, and alderman.

In 1874, the Republican Party nominated him for U.S. Senate, and at the age of 34, he became Mississippi's first black U.S. Senator. He successfully introduced bills which returned millions of dollars to black investors in the Freedman's Savings and Trust Company. However, his other bills to desegregate the army, to support black education, to help the causes of Indians and Orientals, and to give back pay to black soldiers and sailors of the confederate army were always voted down by the Democrat (Dixiecrat) majority.

In 1880, Bruce chaired the Republican Convention, where he supported Grant for President. Bruce recognized Ohio delegate James Garfield, whose support for Grant won him the nomination. Bruce himself was nominated for Vice-president, and received several votes.

His Senate term ended in 1881, after which he worked as Registrar of the Treasury, and Recorder of Deeds. He refused a ministerial appointment to Brazil because that country still had slavery.

He lived well on lecture fees, investments, and his real-estate agency until his death in 1898. He was praised for his "tireless zeal" and "unconquerable ambition." His great service to all humanity earned him the respect of his peers.

Chapter 7
She walked for herself!

Biddy Mason was born a slave around 1820, owned by a man named Robert Smith. She spent the first 30 years of her life on his plantation in Mississippi.

Suddenly, Mr. Smith announced he wanted to travel to Utah. For several months, Biddy walked behind the wagon train tending cattle. During these months she heard strange stories about places to the north where black people were not slaves. She even saw free blacks, and met black families heading west with their own wagons and cattle. She had never seen or heard anything like this and she thought, "I've walked all the way from Mississippi; I've spent my whole life walking for Mr. Smith. Someday I'm going to walk for ME!"

When they arrived in Utah, Mr. Smith and his family decided to go to a settlement in the new state of California.

Biddy loved California, which did not allow slavery, and she was determined somehow to stay as a free woman.

14

For three years the Smith's stayed in California—hiding the fact that they had slaves, and then Mr. Smith decided to move to Texas. Biddy decided she had to act now.

Somehow she got word to the local sheriff that the Smith party leaving for Texas had slaves. When they were getting ready to go, the Sheriff stopped Mr. Smith and said, "We hear you have slaves in your group. Is that true?"

Biddy was afraid, but for the first time in her life, she spoke up to a white man. She ran up to the Sheriff and said, "It's true. Mr. Smith is taking all of us to Texas, and we don't want to go!"

This statement led to one of the hallmark slavery cases involving State's Rights. Did the state of California have to honor Mississippi's slave ownership laws, or did California have the right to enforce its 'no slavery' laws on people from another state? State's Rights won, and it was ruled that slaves from other states could not be considered private property in California. Thereafter, any slave-owner who took his slave to a "free" state, risked losing his "ownership" and having his slave freed.

The judge freed all of Mr. Smith's slaves, and Mr. Smith was heavily fined and asked to leave California.

Biddy settled in Los Angeles, and became a nurse. She saved her money and became one of the wealthiest women in that city dealing in investments and real estate. She then gave land to build schools, hospitals, and nursing homes.

Biddy Mason did indeed walk for herself.

Chapter 8
America's First Black Doctor?

Circa 1500: A young African boy is captured and sold to a Spanish explorer. He is named Estevan, and travels with about 300 other men to explore the newly acquired territory of Florida for the King of Spain.

They reach Florida, and for months they march through jungles and swamps. They have very little food, and mosquitoes, poisonous snakes, and deadly diseases are everywhere. Local Indians attack the travelers. Many men die.

Finally, those who were still alive decided to make rafts and try to sail to Spanish settlements in Mexico. Most of the rafts were lost, but the raft carrying Estevan, his master, and about a dozen others crashed into the coast near the present border of Louisiana and Texas. The men were trapped and enslaved by Indians in the area, and were forced to labor for their captors for more than five years. Their life was so hard, that by then, only 4 men were still alive: Estevan, his master, and 2 Spanish soldiers. They agreed to escape, and after meeting in a pre-arranged place, they fled into the night.

They were free! But they were all alone on the Texas plains. No maps, food, tools, or shelter. Their only hope was to find a Spanish settlement. During their captivity they had learned much about survival from the Indians, but most importantly, Estevan (who had a special talent for this) had picked up several Indian languages.

Heading west before the winter set in, the travelers arrived at a friendly Indian village. The Indians asked if they knew any medicine, and wanted them to heal their sick.

The men had no medical training, but again, Estevan had observed their former captors medical techniques, and successfully applied them. Soon the news of their successes traveled from tribe to tribe, so as the men traveled, they were warmly welcomed by other villages along the way.

Estevan spoke with the people, learning new languages along the way. He found out about lands and villages nearby, and eventually constructed maps and commentary about their travels.

They walked for more than a year, and covered over 1000 miles. Finally in March 1536, they met a group of Spanish soldiers. Their journey was over.

The four men were treated as heroes, but Estevan's abilities captured the attention of the Spanish authorities. The King of Spain hired Estevan as a guide for future explorers. Eventually Estevan led expeditions throughout what is now the southwestern United States making him the first non-Indian to explore the areas of Arizona and New Mexico.

The Zuni Indians of New Mexico have a monument honoring the brave black man who entered their village and healed their sick.

Chapter 9
Color Barrier

After the Civil War, freed Blacks immediately began succeeding in all areas. Successful Black bankers, lawyers, congressmen and restaurateurs were so plentiful, (in Mississippi alone, Blacks almost had a monopoly on the catering business), that the Southern Democrats or "Dixiecrats" began to enforce what became known as Jim Crow laws. (A kind of 'affirmative action' for the southern white minority.) They were jealous of the overnight success of many blacks and felt they had not "paid their dues." The goal was to stomp out successful blacks in all areas of life.

This was also true in baseball. Everyone knows that Jackie Robinson broke down the color barrier in Major League baseball, but not many know the history of how that color barrier came to be—or who Moses "Fleetwood" Walker was.

Much of American baseball was integrated (and international) in the mid 1800s, but the Democrat's Jim Crow laws made it increasingly difficult for teams with black (or Cuban) players to travel in the south because of hotel and transportation difficulties, and unruly spectators. Attempts to ban blacks from playing failed, until the National League in 1876 agreed not to accept any *new* teams which had one or more black players. They would, of course, uphold all prior contracts. However, the extra pressure now on teams with black players, (plus resentment by new teammates), reduced the number of black players to about one dozen by the mid 1880's. Only the best and most indispensable players survived.

Then in 1887, the finest black baseball players of the day were dropped. Newark got rid of their star pitcher, Stovey. Binghamton let their best hitter, Bud Fowler, go. Two new players on the Buffalo Bisons refused to be photographed with their star pitcher, Bob Higgins, who left in mid-season. Finally, in 1889, the only Black playing in Major League Baseball was Moses "Fleetwood" Walker, and Newark did not renew his contract for the following season.

Although he had a batting average of only .212, Moses was famous as one of the greatest bare-hands catchers of his day. One of his new teammates, Pitcher Tony Mullane, who resented Walker said, "He was the best catcher I ever worked with, but I disliked a Negro, and whenever I had to pitch to him, I used anything I wanted without looking at his signals." It would be 57 years before another Black-American would play Major League Baseball.

After that, only a few exhibition games with all-black teams were played, and by 1892 the color barrier was firmly in place.

Moses "Fleetwood" Walker eventually published a newspaper in Steubenville, Ohio called "The Equator". He also owned and operated an Opera house in Cadiz, Ohio and received many patents for inventions relating to the motion picture industry. He died in Cleveland in 1924 at the age of 67.

Chapter 10
Oliver Cromwell

Over 5000 Black soldiers fought side by side with whites in the Revolutionary War. One of the few soldiers, black or white, that fought from the beginning to the end of the war, was a Black-American by the name of Oliver Cromwell.

Oliver was sitting in front of his house in Burlington, NJ enjoying his one-hundredth birthday, when a reporter walked by on East Union Street. The veteran's memory was still very clear, although the last battle at Yorktown had been fought seventy-one years earlier. Oliver told the reporter about enlisting as a private in the 2nd New Jersey Militia commanded by Colonel Israel Shreve. He remembered the long retreats before the British from New York through New Jersey and Pennsylvania. He suffered the bitter winters at Valley Forge and Morristown. He was involved with the crossing of the Delaware surprise attack on Trenton, and later at Princeton where "...we knocked the

British about lively."

He then fought beside General Washington in victories at Brandywine, Monmoouth, and finally Yorktown.

The old man then proudly showed the reporter his honorable discharge signed by Washington in June, 1783 for soldiering for more than six years. The discharge proved that he had won the Badge of Merit—given only to those men who had fought the entire war.

Oliver Cromwell died in January, 1853.

Chapter 11
George Washington Bush

George Washington Bush was a successful Black trapper and furrier who worked throughout the Pacific Northwest from the 1790's to the 1810's. He then took his wealth and settled in Missouri with his wife Isabelle.

Unfortunately, there were many pressures in Missouri because Isabelle was white, so he finally decided to move his family and property to the Oregon territory.

He got a job as a guide for a wagon train going west, so he took his family and belongings and led the group for many months, and over 2000 miles, through deserts and Rocky Mountain blizzards.

One week before they reached their destination, they received word that Oregon had just voted that no Blacks would be allowed to settle there. George had no place to go, except the Washington territory—which was privately owned by the Hudson Bay Company and, until now, only had English settlers.

Four families from the Caravan, along with two other men, chose to follow George and his family, and try and set up a community in the Washington territory—the first United States citizens to settle there.

In 1845, both England and the United States claimed ownership of the Washington territory. It was finally decided that since George Bush and his party were the first non-commercial settlers there, the United States would acquire control of the territory.

George Washington Bush became one of the founders of the State of Washington, and his son, William Owen Bush was elected one of the first Senators in the new State's government.

George died in 1863. The area where they settled is now known as Bush Prairie.

Chapter 12
Robert Smalls

On a dark spring night in Charleston, South Carolina in 1862, the Officers of the Confederate warship, *Planter*, had gone ashore for R&R. Meanwhile, a black crewman by the name of Robert Smalls was hijacking their ship in an attempt to escape to the north. Robert's wife and children had been smuggled aboard, and in an amazing feat of piloting, Robert sailed the ship out of Confederate waters into Union hands. The ship was worth more than $60,000 at that time, and Smalls became a Union hero.

A Union officer wrote, "This man Smalls is superior to any who have come into our lines..." and rewarded him $1500. The Union appointed him a ship pilot in the US Navy. Later when his captain panicked under fire, Smalls took the helm again. Because of this, he was then promoted to Captain and later to Fleet Commander.

Robert Smalls was born in 1839 to a slave by the name of Lydia Smalls. As a slave he served as a waiter, lamplighter, horse driver, rigger, and seaman. He married Hannah Jones at 18, and had 2 daughters, and later a son who died at the age of 3 from smallpox.

After the civil war, the Smalls returned to Beaufort and bought the house where he and his mother had been slaves; and in the process, rescued his former master from bankruptcy. He then began a political career, and in 1868 became a State Representative.

In 1875, he was elected to the United States House of Representatives, and served until 1887. During this time he was harassed constantly by Democrats who claimed he was trying to reclaim South Carolina for Black Republicans.

He lost his seat in 1878 because of voter harassment and cheating, and his 1880 re-election was not confirmed until late in the term. When he lost again in 1886, he did not have the resources to prove the results fraudulent.

After his wife died in 1883, he did not remarry until 1890. His new wife was Annie Wigg, and they had a son, William Robert Smalls.

In 1895, Robert Smalls was one of six Blacks at the State's Republican Convention. Despite his efforts, the Democrats regained power, and once again used their resources in an attempt to disenfranchise blacks with their Jim Crow laws.

The young slave had become a war hero and a champion for his people—and his country—in Congress.

Chapter 13
"The Emporium"

Alonzo Herndon was born a slave in southern Georgia, and was seven years old when the Civil War ended. As a child, he got work as a lumberjack, and them moved on to field hand work on the farm of his former owner. He was paid $50 a year, and supplemented his low wages by selling peanuts, molasses, novelty items, and haircuts—which became his primary income.

He moved to Atlanta with the goal of opening "the finest barbershop in the world." Although he proudly announced his desire to be rich, his real mission in life was "to raise Black America from economic stagnation." Having saved and reinvested his earnings, he opened "The Emporium" in 1904.

With exquisite fixtures and French provincial furnishings, "The Emporium" was equipped with 23 chairs, marble floors, and bronze and crystal chandeliers. Herndon's clientele was pampered by six-foot bathtubs, skilled barbers and bootblacks. Customers, both black and white, claimed to feel more pampered in Herndon's shop than in any of his white competitors.

But Herndon was not satisfied. He was already a millionaire with more than enough money for himself and his family for life, and he paid his black employees extremely well, but he still felt he had not accomplished his mission. He told people close to him that, "America is a capitalist county, and I am a capitalist." He felt that the more wealth he accumulated, the more he could spread it through free-enterprise.

Herndon then came to the rescue of 2 local black ministers whose insurance business was on the brink of bankruptcy. Georgia law required all insurance companies to deposit $5000 annually with the state. This effectively prevented most Black or church based businesses from getting off the ground.

Herndon bought the Atlanta Benevolent and Protective Association, writing policies for blacks when it was virtually impossible, because of presumed bad risk, for them to get insurance. He hired black college graduates from Atlanta and Harvard.

Herndon was excited. "Just think—colored men and women offering employment to those of our own race!" By 1911, his company had grown to 84 branch offices and 70,000 policyholders. He changed the name to Atlanta Life Insurance Company, and today it has assets of over $150 million.

In 1913, he told the faculty and students of Tuskegee Institute (where he was a board member) that, "Wealth and creativity go hand in hand. (We) must possess dreams and visions if (we) really desire to do anything in a big way."

Chapter 14
Clara Brown

Clara Brown was born a slave, in Virginia, in 1803. Throughout her life, she was sold many times before she had saved enough money to buy her freedom.

She heard of the gold that blacks and whites were discovering out west, so at the age of 59, she got a job as a cook for a wagon train of miners heading to Colorado.

Two months later, she arrived in Denver where she immediately started a Sunday School and a laundry business. She decided, though, that the big money was in the mining towns, so she moved to Central City.

There she did very well, and in addition to starting Sunday Schools and Bible studies, she soon managed to save $10,000 from her laundry earnings, and investments in mining shares. While she was wondering what to do with her savings, she heard the news that the War Between the States was over, and that the Union had won. For the rest of her life, she devoted her resources to helping Black

Americans travel west, and to searching for her lost relatives. She found a total of 34 distant relatives, and helped all of them.

She became a wealthy and well-respected leading citizen of Central City, and, before her death in 1885, one last dream came true. Her daughter, who had been sold while she was still in Virginia, finally found her.

Chapter 15
James Forten

During the Revolutionary War, an American Warship by the name of *Royal Louis* set out to sea to ambush and destroy British vessels. Out of a crew of two hundred, twenty were black. One by the name of James Forten was in charge of Ammunition and Powder aboard the *Royal Louis*.

James was born in Philadelphia and attended one of the many Quaker schools there. At fifteen, he signed up as a drummer in the army. Later, he transferred to the Navy and was assigned the *Royal Louis*. After many successful raids, the Royal Louis was forced to surrender to the British warship, *Amphyon*, and two other vessels.

The British did not keep black POWs, but instead sold them as slaves in the West Indies. Somehow, James befriended the British Captain's son who was very impressed with James' wit—and his skill at playing marbles. James later wrote, "Thus did a game of marbles save me from a life of West Indian servitude."

The son persuaded his father to offer James a life of ease and freedom in England, but James refused, saying, "No. I'm a prisoner for my country, and I'll never be a traitor to her."

As a result James was sent with other prisoners to the prison ship, *Jersey,* anchored off Long Island. Thousands of American POWs were held in the hold of this ship and forced to eat wormy meat and foul water in smelly and overcrowded conditions. Every day the British would collect the dead, and during the course of the War, over 10,000 Americans died on this ship and were buried in the sand dunes off of Long Island.

After seven months, James was released as part of a prisoner exchange program, and returned to his native Philadelphia. As a war hero, he became very well known in his community, and soon developed a successful business making and repairing sails.

He employed scores of people, and also patented many inventions.

He used much of his wealth as one of the founders of the abolitionist movement. In 1833, his daughter, Margaretta, founded the "Female Anti-Slavery Society" in Philadelphia.

He never regretted his life as a drummer, powder man, or prisoner. When asked about the Revolutionary War, he said, "The spirit of Freedom is marching with rapid strides and causing Tyrants to tremble."

Chapter 16
Mission Impossible

Sometime in the late fall of 1848, a young man stylishly dressed in a black suit and cape, high-heeled boots, and green-tinted sunglasses, boarded a steamer going from Savannah, Georgia, to Charleston, South Carolina. He was traveling to Philadelphia to have dental work done, and as a result, his head and face were covered with a toothache bandage. His right arm was in a sling, so the male slave who was accompanying him had to cut his food, feed him, and do his talking for him.

The gentleman dined at the Captain's table, and was told, "You got a real nice boy there, but be careful when you get up north; they can turn on you real quick. And watch out for those damned abolitionists!"

What the Captain did not know was that the young gentleman was really Ellen Craft, an escaped slave, who was accompanied by her husband, another escaped slave from a different Georgia plantation. Although she had a light complexion, the bandage disguised the fact that she had no beard, and she wore the sling because she could not write. She only nodded when spoken to, because her voice would give her away, and her husband would quickly explain the toothache, answer questions, and apologize for his "master". Her husband had raised enough money from odd mechanic jobs to afford the stylish clothing and the journey. They were trying to get far enough north to make contact with the Underground Railroad (which did not extend down into Georgia). But one slip, and they would be hung.

They took a train to Richmond, where they registered at a hotel. Her husband, William Craft, did all the talking, explaining that he needed to stay with his master because of his obvious handicaps and ailments.

When they reached Baltimore, they were informed that a slave could not get a ticket without a written guarantee from his master. William cried and pleaded, saying his master was in such pain, could not write, and had to get to the dental surgeon in Philadelphia as soon as possible—it was an emergency. His master might die on the way if they did not board now. The ticket master waived the rule, and sold them the two tickets.

When they arrived in Philadelphia, they were taken care of by friends, and Ellen had to recuperate in bed for several days because of the emotional strain. They were then assisted on to Boston, because slave catchers knew that Philadelphia was a harbor for runaways.

The Crafts later were highly paid guest speakers at antislave meetings and rallies as they told their incredible story of escape. They later traveled to England with the story of how they had devised their escape plan and successfully carried it out.

Chapter 17
Rev. John Jasper

Sometime in June of 1839, a seventeen-year-old slave by the name John Jasper began preaching Sundays on the plantation of John Blair Peachy in Richmond, Virginia.

His incredible oratory and ingenious speaking style became so renown, that a white man by the name of Dr. Cecil Winfree invited him to speak at a family member's funeral. He was to follow a white preacher.

When he got to the Winfree plantation, the white preacher refused to let Jasper speak. When Jasper insisted that Dr. Winfree had requested him, the white preacher made fun of him to the crowd; and then spoke for two and a half hours in hopes that Jasper would give up and leave. Finally Dr. Winfree demanded that Jasper speak, and the white preacher snidely said, "Now, you'll hear some ni**er logic."

Facing a mocking crowd, Jasper spoke with such eloquence and vivid word pictures, that by the end of his

30-minute sermon, the crowd was cheering, and begged him to come preach next Sunday. He politely declined saying he had already promised to preach in Charles City.

After that he was in great demand for funerals and sermons, but more remarkably, his own plantation church became so huge, that a new building was built. He also developed a large number of white parishioners who came regularly—but had to sit in the 'Whites Only' section because of Jim Crow Laws.

When Pastor Benjamin Kean, of a white church in Petersburg, began to miss some of his congregation, he asked his deacons, who said, "They're down the road in the Old Third Church listening to Rev. John Jasper." Dr. Kean said, "*Reverend* Jasper? He can't be a minister. God never ordains Negroes."

Dr. Kean took three of his deacons to a Sunday afternoon meeting, and sure enough, there was his wayward flock. When Jasper saw them, he smiled warmly and said, "Look here, you'all white folk; don't get in the seats of the regular customers."

Ten minutes later, Dr. Kean and his deacons were in tears, praising God. They totally forgot they were listening to a black man. Dr. Kean later said, "Thank God! He *does* ordain Negroes!"

After the Civil War, Jasper was finally free to get a denominational church of his own, and on September 3, 1867 he organized the "Sixth Mount Zion Baptist Church." When asked if there had been five earlier Mount Zions, he said, "No. We just liked the way the name sounded."

One of Jasper's most famous sermons was titled "The Sun Do Move!" This sermon was such a success, that the Richmond Whig advertised, "Sunday, March 28, 1878, John Jasper will preach at 3:00 PM on "The Sun Do Move!" Thousands came to hear this sermon, and over the next several years he delivered this sermon over two hundred and fifty times. He then made a tour through Baltimore, Washington, Philadelphia, and New York. Whenever it was advertised for 3:00, people would say, "Yes, the service is at 3 P.M. but if you wish to see the church at all, you best be there by 12:00."

He continued to pastor the Sixth Mount Zion Baptist Church for thirty-three and a half years until his death, March 28, 1901. At the peak of his ministry in the 1880s, he had over 2000 parishioners—almost one-third of who were white. His last words - written on his tombstone were, "I have finished my work. I am waiting at the river, looking across for further orders."

"The iniquity of slavery can never be obliterated without 'the mind of Christ'. Unaided human thinking at its highest, as seen in Aristotle, defends bondage on the grounds of race diversity: 'Mankind is divisible into the free, and the slaves by nature.'

"But the Man of Galilee took the Slave by one hand, and the Owner by the other, set them face to face and said, 'You are brothers.'"

John Jasper

Chapter 18
James T. Rapier

James T. Rapier was born in Florence, Alabama to a black lady named Susan in 1837. They managed to escape to Canada where he received his education. He then studied law at the University of Glasgow in Scotland. When the Civil war broke out, he returned to the United States to help the Union as a war correspondent for a pro-North newspaper. He was working behind Confederate lines in Tennessee when the Union Army captured Nashville.

His law studies enabled him to be admitted to the Tennessee bar, and a few years later, he was the keynote speaker at the Tennessee Negro Suffrage Convention, and a delegate to the state Constitutional Convention in 1865.

Eventually, he returned home to Florence and became a successful cotton farmer. Because of his reputation for success in Tennessee, he was invited to the Alabama state

House to help write its constitution. His desire for a political voice for Black-Americans led him to become the co-founder of the Alabama's Republican Party. As a result, he became a target of the Ku Klux Klan, and fled for his life and remained in hiding in Montgomery for over a year.

Two years later, he became the Republican candidate for Secretary of State, but lost the election to a white man.

In 1870 he was elected vice-president of the National Negro Labor Union, and president of the Alabama Negro Labor Union. In 1872, he won a seat in the US congress, defeating a former Confederate Officer. He was appointed to the labor committee where he worked hard *against* minimum wage laws which were designed to keep blacks out of the job market.

He returned to farming until tuberculosis took him home in 1883.

Chapter 19
Black Wealth Generator

We usually associate the Fuller Products Company with images of white salesmen who traveled rural America from the 40's through the 60's. What is not generally known is the great wealth these salesmen were generating for thousands of black families throughout America.

The Fuller Products Company was founded by a black man named S. B. Fuller. He was born in 1905 in Ouachita Parish, Louisiana, and the oldest of eight children. At age nine he had a job driving mules, and he quit school after the sixth grade. His father left when he was seventeen, and the family moved to Memphis.

He often wondered, "Why are some people wealthy and others poor?" On her deathbed, his mother told him, "We shouldn't be poor, son, and don't let me ever hear you say it's God's will. We're poor only because Father never developed the desire for anything else."

S.B. hitchhiked to Chicago in 1928 and held a variety of sales jobs. He finally settled on Insurance, and did very well until he saw a published list of the wealthiest men in Chicago. In 1934 the President of Chicago Metropolitan Life earned $50,000, while the head of Lever Brothers (a local soap company) earned nine times that much.

With $25 in his pocket, S.B. immediately became a distributor for National Laboratories selling soap and other toiletries door to door. When his supplier had difficulties paying him in a timely manner, he vowed that someday he would own the company. Ten years later, he had saved enough, and *did* buy the company. He then saved an additional $25,000 dollars and started The Fuller Products Company.

He re-settled in Louisiana, and set up sales forces of mostly black men throughout the south. He was harassed by the Klan, accused of exploitation, and constantly attacked with frivolous legislation. In spite of this, his sales grew astronomically, and black families who sold for him began to develop serious wealth. He used a networking system of distribution, and his initial salesmen earned overrides and company profit sharing.

When his sales force expanded into the mid-west by the 1950s, S.B. Fuller was declared one of the wealthiest men in America. His economic empire eventually grew to include the Courier Newspaper Chain (with papers in Pittsburgh, New York, Detroit, and Chicago), a Chicago department store, and a New York real estate trust. Through his various enterprises, he is probably responsible for single-handedly creating more wealth and economic freedom for Black-American families than any other person, company, or organization.

His incredible success almost came to an abrupt halt in 1963 when the NAACP approached him and asked for some of his hard-earned millions. He declined, saying that he believed he was more capable of using his money for the betterment of America's Black citizens than they were. When the civil rights organization continued to harass him, he made a speech to the National Association of Manufacturers addressing his concerns. His speech read, in part:

It is contrary to the laws of nature for man to stand still: He must move forward or the eternal march of progress will force him backward. This the Negro has failed to understand. He believes that the lack of civil rights legislation and the lack of integration have kept him back. But this is not true.... In 1952, the Negro's income was 57% of that of the white man's, but in 1962 it was only 53% of his income. In a period of ten years, the Negro's income has dropped four percentage points in comparison with the white man's income. The main reason for this is the Negro's lack of understanding of our capitalist system of government....

Unfortunately, the Negro believes that there is a racial barrier in America which keeps him from succeeding, yet if he would learn to use the laws of observation, concentration, memory, reason, and action, he would realize that there is a world of opportunity right in his own community. Since the Negro does not supply the demand in his own community, the white man must come in, and he takes advantage of the opportunity. Then the Negro thinks that there is a racial barrier that keeps him from making progress. Therefore, he asks for legislation to remove the barrier which he automatically created himself, due to the lack of action on his own behalf.

As a result of Fuller's refusal to hand over his money, the NAACP called for a nation-wide boycott of all of

Fuller's businesses. They also called for investigations, charging him with violations of several provisions of the Federal Securities Act.

What the Klan, Jim Crow, abusive power, and frivolous litigation could not do, the Civil Rights industry almost succeeded in doing. Fuller barely escaped bankruptcy, but fortunately his sales forces, employees, and the hundreds of thousands of individuals and families who had benefited from his industry came to his defense, and his companies still stand successful today; benefiting all Americans.

Chapter 20
Our First Black Congressman

Joseph Hayne Rainey was born a slave in 1832, in Georgetown, South Carolina. His father's successful barbering business allowed the family to purchase their freedom.

When the Civil war broke out, the Confederacy drafted Rainey to work on military fortifications in the Charleston harbor.

After the fall of the South, Rainey entered politics and was elected to the State House and Senate. In 1870, he was elected to the U.S. House of Representatives, becoming the first Black to be seated.

The Ku Klux Klan was founded in 1866 by Southern Democrats as a secret terrorist society. Its goal was the restoration of White supremacy in the southern states and the intimidation of any Black seeking political office. Rep.

Rainey helped to draft federal legislation in 1871 to severely curb Klan activities. As a result, Federal troops occupied South Carolina and other southern states, capturing hundreds of Klan leaders, and forcing many to flee.

Rainey always pointed out that the newly freed Black majority in southern states did *not* take advantage of the white minority. He is quoted as saying, "Our state convention which met in 1868, and in which Negroes were in a large majority, did not pass any proscriptive or disenfranchising acts, but adopted a liberal constitution, securing alike equal rights to all citizens, White and Black, male and female as far as possible."

In May of 1874, Rainey achieved another Black first. During the House speaker's absence, Rainey presided over the house as Speaker. Toni Morrison has declared President Clinton as America's first Black president, but in May of 1874, when the President was overseas, and the vice-president was severely ill, Representative Rainey had full Presidential powers.

After leaving Congress, Rainey opened a banking and brokerage firm. He and his wife later retired to Georgetown, South Carolina, where he died at the young age of 55 in 1887. He was a trailblazer and a noble warrior in battles against overwhelming odds.

Chapter 21
George H. White

After the Civil war, more than 20 Black Americans represented their constituents by serving in the U.S. House or Senate between 1870 and 1898.

The last of these was a man named George H. White. He was born in Rosindale, North Carolina to a family that farmed and made barrels. He entered Howard University at age 21, and worked his way through college by teaching and tutoring. He then passed the bar exam and opened a law office in New Bern, NC, in 1879.

He had several successful runs in the State Senate, and then in 1894, he ran for the US. House of Representatives. He lost in the Republican primary to his brother-in-law Henry Cheatham, who won the race. In 1896, he ran again, and was elected by a large majority of both black and white voters. He was re-elected in 1898 (after a vicious name-calling campaign), which made him the last Black American to serve in the US Congress in the 19th century.

George White had seen the whole discouraging story: the Black entrance into political power after the Civil War, and the loss of that power to undermining Southern Democrats and their Jim Crow laws. When he left Congress in 1901, the reconstruction era of Black political power was over, but in his parting speech he said:

"You may tie us and then taunt us for a lack of bravery, but one day we will break the bonds. You may use our labor for two and a half centuries, and then taunt us for our poverty, but let me remind you, we will not always remain poor. You may withhold even the knowledge of how to read God's word and learn the way of the earth to glory, and then taunt us for our ignorance, but we would remind you that there is plenty of room at the top, and we are climbing.

This, Mr. Chairman, is perhaps the Negroes' temporary farewell to the American Congress, but let me say, Phoenix-like, he will rise up some day and come again. These parting words are in behalf of an outraged, heartbroken, bruised and bleeding, but God-fearing, faithful, industrious, loyal people—full of potential force."

It would be 27 years before this prophecy would come true and another Black American would serve the US in the House of Representatives. In 1928, the Republican Party nominated Oscar S. DePriest, who became a Representative for the state of Illinois.

George White died in 1918, after setting up large trust funds for Black Families to enable them to buy houses and farms on easy-payment terms arranged by White.

Chapter 22
Not so famous quotations:

"There is a class of...people who make a business of keeping the troubles, the wrongs, and the hardships of the Negro race before the public. Having learned that they are able to make a living out of their troubles, they have grown into the settled habit of advertising their wrongs...because it pays. Some of these people do not want the Negro to lose his grievances—because they do not want to lose their jobs."

Booker T. Washington

"I'd rather be in jail in America than free anywhere else."

Eldridge Cleaver

"Welfare is the first step back toward slavery."

*"The greatest enemy of the Black Man
is the White liberal."*

Malcolm X

Chapter 23
Black Progress in America
(Essay)

Democrats fought a bloody war in an attempt to keep slavery legal. When they lost, they instituted the Ku Klux Klan in 1866 to terrorize Black Republicans who were nominated for public office. When this failed, they started the Jim Crow Laws in an attempt to disenfranchise the newly successful Black population.

In spite of all this, Black Americans kept prospering, so in desperation, Democrats instituted a eugenics program to "sterilize the poor and colored". This initiative was headed by Margaret Sanger, who later went on to found Planned Parenthood which now oversees the majority of abortions in this country; abortions where one out of three result in the death of a black baby. Genocide?

Democrats finally found a chance during the Great Depression when President FDR shipped leftover food and seed (unused by white farmers) and *sold* them to Black communities in exchange for votes. This allowed Democrats to take the Black vote for granted ever since.

However, Blacks continued to prosper and discover their American Dream, so in a last desperate attempt to keep Blacks down-trodden, de-humanized, and dependent, Democrats developed a drug called welfare.

Malcolm X remembers his mother boiling grass to eat so that they could refuse welfare. He said, "Welfare is the first step back to slavery."

However, continued Black success caused Democrats to start the "Great Society" which set up ghettos to keep "undesirables away from descent folk" in housing projects.

There were more Republicans (82%) than Democrats (69%) who voted *for* the Civil Right Initiative in 1964. (Opposing Democrats included Senator Al Gore Sr. from Tennessee). After the bill passed, President Lyndon Johnson told his Black driver that, "No matter what laws are passed, you'll still be a ni**er."

Democrats have been in charge of our major cities now for almost 40 years, and have presided over the destruction of our schools, our families, our property (through taxes), our businesses, our neighborhoods, and our opportunities. They have tried to keep us uneducated, poor, and feeling like helpless victims who can't make it without Democrat help. Why? Because if we became educated, prosperous, and independent, we wouldn't need them and might vote Republican.

"There's nothing more dangerous to liberalism
than an educated Black Man"

Jon Saboe
1998

Chapter 24
Racism In The Public Schools
(Essay)

During our country's dark chapter of slavery, there were many attempts to justify the inhuman treatment and degradation of fellow Americans. One was the abuse and perversion of Article 1, Section 2 of our constitution leading to the "three-fifths" laws, which implicitly declared blacks to be 3/5 human. There were attempts to convince others that "Negroes didn't feel pain." Blacks were taught that they were sub-human, and many dictionaries of the early 1800s contained the word 'sub-human' in their definition of 'negro'.

The root philosophy found in these attempts is one of 'dehumanization'. Before a populace can be convinced to endorse atrocities, they must first be convinced that the victims are not fully human. This was true for the Jews in Nazi Germany, the Aborigines of Australia, and the unborn in many developed nations.

Although our educational systems have made great strides in the areas of Human Rights, and the dignity of 'All People', there is still one vestigial philosophy which pervades our governmental education system and affects our children and our students at many levels.

This philosophical system is one in which the veneer of 'Science' is given to the institution of racism, and the resulting atrocities are often not heard of.

"Scientists" hunted and killed thousands of Australian Aboriginals in an attempt to study "the missing link", which is what Aboriginals were believed to be. Skins, skulls, and bones were taken from live humans and placed in laboratories and museums in England, the United States, and around the world. Children were stolen from their parents in an attempt to "uplift" them into "superior" society.

As recently as 1906, a captured pygmy was on exhibit in the Bronx Zoo in New York's Zoological Park. He was caged with an orangutan, and visitors were encouraged to find similarities.[1]

The acknowledged founder of this philosophical system, which is still being taught exclusively today, used the term "Anthropomorphous Apes" to describe Negroes and people of African Descent to portray them as only mimicking humanity:

"At some future period...the civilized races of man will almost certainly exterminate and replace the savage races throughout the world.. At the same time the

---

[1]See *One Blood: The Biblical Answer to Racism*, Master Books. 1999

anthropomorphous apes will no doubt be exterminated.
The break between man and his nearest allies will then be wider, for it will intervene between man (in a more civilized state, as we may hope, even than the Caucasian), and some ape as low as a baboon, instead of as now between the negro or Australian and the gorilla."

This statement, which appears to look forward to a future race war, appears on page 178 in the book "The Descent of Man" which was published in 1874 and written by Charles Darwin. Although we are certainly horrified by this quote, the fact remains that his philosophies concerning human origins are taught as scientific fact throughout our country.

The late Professor of Zoology and Paleontology at Harvard University, Dr. Stephen Jay Gould said the following:

"Biological arguments for racism may have been common before 1859, but they increased by orders of magnitude following the acceptance of evolutionary theory."

Evolutionary philosophy or "naturalism" is accepted as science throughout our educational facilities, yet it has its foundation in the prejudices and 'sciences' of the 1800s. Why is something so inherently racist allowed to be unchallenged?

As said before, human rights are easily violated when people are convinced that the victims are not fully human. In the case of slavery, an attempt was made to dehumanize African-Americans. In the case of naturalism, the attempt is made to dehumanize all of humanity – the ultimate racism against the human race!

During slavery, blacks were taught that they were sub-human. *Now* our children are being taught that they are not human at all, but animals! If children are taught that they are nothing more than animals, they will start to behave like animals. They will kill those who get in their way, prowl and stalk females for sex, and adopt a 'law of the jungle' mentality in dealing with society. After two to three generations of evolutionary indoctrination, it is not surprising to see an increase in youth violence, teenage pregnancies, and tragedies like Columbine. (As a man thinks in his heart, so is he.)

Our Constitution states that our rights are endowed by our Creator, and even an atheist has to admit that the preeminent legal document of our land declares that our rights come from God. This is legal justification for teaching our children that they are "Created in the image of God" which is fundamental to all of the world's great monotheistic religions.

Two additional quotes from Charles Darwin show how backward and anti-social his philosophies are:

Concerning Women:

"The chief distinction in the intellectual powers of the two sexes is shown by man attaining to a higher eminence (in whatever he takes up) than woman can attain; whether requiring deep thought, reason, or imagination, or merely the use of the senses and hands." ('The Descent of Man', vol. II, p. 327)

Concerning Health-care:

"Vaccination has preserved thousands, who from a weak constitution would formerly have succumbed to smallpox. Thus the weak members of civilized societies propagate their kind.

This must be highly injurious to the race of man. It is surprising how soon a want of care, or care wrongly directed, leads to the degeneration of a domestic race.

We must bear without complaining the undoubtedly bad effects of the weak surviving and propagating their kind."
('The Descent of Man', vol. I, p. 168-9)

Attempts were made to sterilize "Poor and Black" women in the 1920s in an attempt to improve the human species through eugenics. The founder of this movement, Margaret Sanger, went on to establish "Planned Parenthood" where one out of every three aborted babies is Black. (Genocide?) Just another of the sanctioned atrocities built upon the naturalistic philosophies of evolution.

How is it that a dead, racist, European philosophy continues to flourish in the United States of America?

We need to rid our schools of any and all philosophies which have their basis in racist or supremacist thought. We would certainly not allow the use of *'Mein Kampf'* as a basis for our curricula, but we allow and defend the philosophies of Charles Darwin, Aldous Huxley and John Dewy, all of which encourage the belief that "some are more evolved than others".

If our children were taught that they (and their peers) were "made in the image of God", they might think twice before stealing, killing or raping. There would be some kind of deterrent as they were forced to ask themselves, "Is that person a Child of God, or just a collection of random chemicals?"

Let's try and restore our country's schools to the American ideal that "All people are created equal" and denounce the European philosophies of Naturalism, Evolutionism, and "Survival of the Fittest".

Jon Saboe
1999

Bibliography/Suggested Reading

Bennett, Lerone. *Before the Mayflower*. Penguin Books. 1988

Davis, Burke. *Black Heroes of the American Revolution.* Harcourt Brace & Co. 1976

Green, Richard L. *A Salute to Blacks in the Federal Government.* Empak Publishing Company. 1990

Ham, Ken; Wieland, Carl; Battan, Don. One Blood: *The Biblical Answer to Racism.* Master Books. 1999

Haskins, Jim. *Get on Board.* Scholastic Inc. 1993

Johnson, James "Johnny". *Beyond Defeat.* ISBN 038513486x 1978

Keyes, Alan K. *Masters of the Dream.* Morrow. 1995

Kimbro, Dennis. *Daily Motivations for African-American*

Success. Fawcett-Crest. 1993

Eldridge Cleaver. *Soul on Fire!* Word Books, 1978

Otis, George. *Eldridge Cleaver: Ice and Fire!* Bible Voice. 1977

Pelz, Ruth. *Black Heroes of the Wild West.* Open Hand Publishing. 1990

Richburg, Keith B. *Out of America.* Basic Books. 1997

Tygiel, Jules. *Baseball's Great Experiment.* Oxford University Press. 1983

Williams, Walter E. *The State Against Blacks.* New Press. 1982

Weaver, Mason. *It's OK To Leave the Plantation.* Unsourced Press. 1997

Woodson, Sr., Robert L. *The Triumphs of Joseph.* The Free Press. 1998

INDEX: